Understanding
Addiction

Melissa Abramovitz

D1606691

ReferencePoint
Press®

San Diego, CA

© 2018 ReferencePoint Press, Inc.
Printed in the United States

For more information, contact:
ReferencePoint Press, Inc.
PO Box 27779
San Diego, CA 92198
www.ReferencePointPress.com

LIBRARY OF CONGRESS CATALOGING-IN-PUBLICATION DATA

Name: Abramovitz, Melissa, 1954– author.
Title: Understanding Addiction/by Melissa Abramovitz.
Description: San Diego, CA: ReferencePoint Press, Inc., 2018. | Series:
  Understanding Psychology | Audience: Grade 9-12. | Includes
  bibliographical references and index.
Identifiers: LCCN 2017021326 (print) | LCCN 2017022146 (ebook) | ISBN
  9781682822722 (eBook) | ISBN 9781682822715 (hardback)
Subjects: LCSH: Compulsive behavior—Juvenile literature. | Substance
  abuse—Juvenile literature. | Compulsive behavior—Treatment—Juvenile
  literature.
Classification: LCC RC533 (ebook) | LCC RC533 .A267 2018 (print) | DDC
  362.29--dc23
LC record available at https://lccn.loc.gov/2017021326

CONTENTS

The Human Brain: Thought, Behavior, and Emotion

Frontal lobe controls:
- Thinking
- Planning
- Organizing
- Problem solving
- Short-term memory
- Movement
- Personality
- Emotions
- Behavior
- Language

Parietal lobe:
- Interprets sensory information such as taste, temperature, and touch

Temporal lobe:
- Processes information from the senses of smell, taste, and hearing
- Plays role in memory storage

Occipital lobe:
- Processes images from the eyes
- Links information with images stored in memory

Source: Mayo Foundation for Education and Research, "Slide Show: How Your Brain Works." www.mayoclinic.org.

INTRODUCTION

The Personal and Social Impact of Addiction

People can be addicted to a variety of substances or behaviors, including drugs, alcohol, gambling, sex, the Internet, eating, and shopping. And all types of addiction have profound physical, emotional, psychological, financial, and social effects. As the National Center on Addiction and Substance Abuse (CASA) website notes, addiction "damages individuals, families, relationships, and every situation in which people live and work."[1] The most serious and widespread effects, however, are associated with substance addictions.

Physical and Emotional Damage

The physical effects of addiction may stem from violence associated with the drug dealers with whom many addicts associate, homelessness, accidents, overdoses, and numerous diseases. The National Institute on Drug Abuse (NIDA) reports that about 90,000 Americans die each year from the consequences of alcohol and drug addiction and abuse (excluding tobacco). Of these deaths, 47,055 resulted from drug overdoses in 2014. An additional 480,000 Americans die each year from the consequences of tobacco addiction, including from cancers and heart disease.

Drug addicts who share syringes to inject drugs also expose themselves to infectious diseases like AIDS and hepatitis. The Centers for Disease Control and Prevention (CDC) reports that about 12 percent of new AIDS cases are caused by injecting heroin, cocaine, or methamphetamine and that one-third of all AIDS deaths are related to drug abuse. In other cases drug

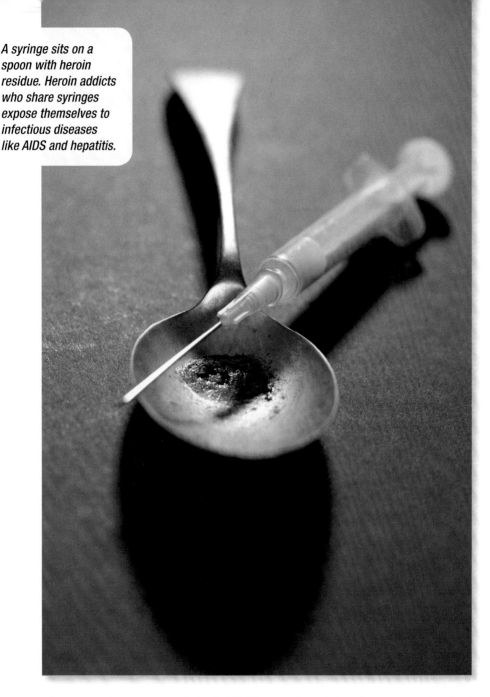

abuse reduces people's inhibitions about having unprotected sex, which also spreads sexually transmitted diseases.

Besides being responsible for many deaths, substance addictions cause or exacerbate physical, mental, and emotional illnesses and disabilities. Indeed, a 2015 study by researchers at the University of Washington found that about 40 percent of people addicted to drugs in the United States have attempted suicide. The Substance Abuse and Mental Health Services Administration (SAMHSA) notes that substance addictions and mental illnesses "are among the top conditions that cause disability. . . . By 2020, mental and substance abuse disorders will surpass all physical diseases as a major cause of disability worldwide."[2]

Effects on Families

The fact that many addicts cannot work or attend to other responsibilities also affects them and their families financially, emotionally, and physically. For example, Kat's addiction to heroin, alcohol, and other drugs prevented her from working and caring for her son. At age sixteen, he finally confronted her because he could no longer tolerate being hungry and taking cold showers (the electric company turned off the power because Kat failed to pay the bills). He told Kat he would alert authorities and ask to be placed in a foster home unless she got help.

In other situations, well-meaning family members exhibit what is known as codependent behavior that supports the addict's actions. For example, psychotherapist Barbara Sinor explains in her book *Tales of Addiction and Inspiration for Recovery* that she and her husband enabled their son Rich's alcoholism by repeatedly bailing him out of jail, giving him money, and allowing him to abuse their hospitality.

Many addicts also actively or passively promote addiction in their children. When Teresa was nine years old, for example, her marijuana-addicted father encouraged her and her siblings to smoke pot at the parties he hosted in their San Francisco–area home. When Teresa ran away from home, she abused alcohol, marijuana, and other drugs because this was the only lifestyle she knew. Children like Teresa often perform poorly in or drop out of school, become sexually promiscuous, and end up in abusive relationships.

Another way in which addiction harms families is that babies born to addicts often have disabilities such as fetal alcohol syndrome, which includes learning, emotional, and physical abnormalities. Children exposed to secondhand cigarette or marijuana smoke are also at vastly increased risk for asthma, heart disease, lung cancer, and other diseases. Indeed, "there is no risk-free level of exposure to secondhand smoke,"[3] according to the CDC.

Effects on Society

Addiction also affects society as a whole. It costs law enforcement, social services, and health care agencies billions of dollars each year; NIDA estimates that drug addictions alone cost taxpayers and affected individuals more than $700 billion each year in the United States. Victims of traffic accidents and other crimes caused by alcoholics and other addicts suffer additional financial, physical, and emotional trauma. In 2014 alone, the CDC notes, nearly ten thousand Americans were killed in car accidents caused by drunk drivers.

The burden on law enforcement and social service agencies is especially weighty and long lasting when teens become addicts. Substance-addicted teens do poorly in school and are at high risk for incarceration, depression, homelessness, and other problems that strain social service networks. Substance abuse and addictions also drive the vast number of nonconsensual sexual encounters among college students and other young people. "One of the more important risk factors for nonconsensual sexual contact is the use of alcohol and drugs,"[4] states a 2015 study funded by the Association of American Universities.

The War on Drugs

The ongoing effects of addiction on individuals, families, and society have led addiction experts and policy makers to call for new approaches to confronting these challenges. Indeed, the consensus is that since President Richard Nixon declared a war on drugs in 1971, the associated policies, which mostly still exist, have failed. For instance, despite increases in the size and reach of drug control agencies, expanded drug education, and mandatory jail time for illegal drug possession, drug use and addiction rates have not diminished. Many experts believe that helping addicts obtain treatment, rather than punishing them, would be more productive.

However, efforts to enhance treatment access, and associated proposals like needle exchanges and legalizing illegal drugs, are controversial. For example, some people believe legalizing illegal drugs would help authorities control the high drug prices that drive many addicts to steal money. But drug legalization is especially controversial since the number of traffic accidents caused by marijuana users in states like Washington that have legalized marijuana have increased.

Authorities do agree, however, that addiction policies should change. As California judge James P. Gray writes in his book *Why Our Drug Laws Have Failed and What We Can Do About It*, "We have never been a drug-free society and we never will be. Recognizing this fact, and recognizing that these harmful drugs are here to stay, we should try to employ an approach that will most effectively reduce the deaths, disease, crime, and misery caused by their presence in our communities."[5]

CHAPTER 1

What Is Addiction?

Addiction is a condition in which an individual wants and needs something so much that he or she is physically and mentally unable to stop consuming a particular substance or engaging in a particular behavior, even though continuing the behavior can be dangerous, unpleasant, and even fatal. As addiction specialist Dr. Drew Pinsky explains, "Excessive drug use chemically tricks the brain so that the pursuit of the drug becomes a higher priority than survival."[6] This applies to other types of addictions as well.

Indeed, all types of addiction include common elements. These include a compulsion to seek and ingest a particular substance or engage in a particular behavior and a need for increasing amounts of the substance or behavior due to habituation, or tolerance. When the addictive substance or behavior overshadows other pastimes and becomes the center of the addict's life, that is another common element of addiction. So are physical and psychological withdrawal symptoms, which may include irritability, restlessness, sleeplessness, nausea, seizures, and other symptoms that occur when the substance or behavior is withdrawn.

Many people mistakenly believe that only substance addictions become involuntary, but this happens with all types of addictions. For example, hundreds of local newspaper articles and reports from the Casino Watch organization confirm that numerous casinos ban certain gambling addicts because these individuals' compulsions are so strong that they lead these people to break child-protection laws. In fact, many of these gambling addicts have left their children unsupervised in a car in a casino parking lot all night or day while they were busy gambling. These children, along with many others whose parents are online gaming addicts, have been placed in foster homes in recent years.

The compulsive nature of addiction results in people with one addiction being very likely to suffer from other addictions. For example, people addicted to alcohol are more likely than those in the general population to become addicted

to drugs like cocaine and nicotine (the drug in tobacco) and are also more susceptible to behavioral addictions like gambling, pornography, and compulsive buying. In fact, studies indicate that about half of all gambling addicts are also addicted to alcohol, and more than half are addicted to nicotine.

People play slot machines in a Las Vegas casino. Compulsions of gambling addicts can be so strong that some will leave their children unsupervised in a casino parking lot all day or all night while they gamble.

Who Is Affected?

Addiction affects millions of people in all age groups, socioeconomic classes, and racial and ethnic groups. In 2017 CASA reported that 40 million Americans aged twelve or older (16 percent of the population) suffered from drug or alcohol addiction—more than the number with heart disease (27 million) or cancer (19 million).

Although many people believe that addicts fit the stereotype of being impoverished, uneducated, and lazy, in truth, addicts of all types come from all walks of life. For example, Jared grew up in a conservative, upper-middle-class family in Kentucky and started abusing alcohol in high school. After earning his degree as a pharmacist, he began stealing and abusing the narcotics in his pharmacy because, in his words, the drugs made him "happier, friendlier, more energetic, funnier, better looking, and downright invincible."[7] He became addicted and was finally arrested for stealing these drugs. In fact, although many people think medical professionals such as doctors, nurses, and pharmacists are too intelligent and successful to become addicts, medical professionals become addicted to prescription drugs more often than other people do because they have easy access to these drugs. For instance, doctors have an estimated 10 percent to 15 percent risk of becoming addicted to prescription narcotics, compared to 9 percent for the rest of the population. When it comes to alcohol and illegal drugs, medical professionals become addicted to these substances about as often as others in the general population.

Diagnosing Addiction

However, not everyone who abuses addictive substances or compulsively engages in certain behaviors is classified as an addict. CASA notes that there is often a fine line between what is considered to be risky substance abuse, which can threaten a user's health, safety, and ability to function, and true addiction, which includes other criteria like compulsions. For example, according to the National Institute on Alcohol Abuse and Alcoholism, a woman who consumes more than three alcoholic drinks in one day or more than seven in one week, and a man who drinks more than four drinks in a day or more than fourteen in a week are considered to have a problem with risky alcohol abuse, but are not necessarily addicts.

Although there are standardized criteria for diagnosing addiction, assessing who is or is not an addict can be difficult. Signs of addiction that experts say should lead to a professional assessment include secretive behaviors; frequent absences from or poor performance in school or work; changes in friends, dress, or habits; severe mood changes; talk of suicide; violent actions; changes in eating or sleeping habits; and loss of interest in one's usual pastimes. In some cases, when addiction coexists with mental disorders like depression, schizophrenia, or bipolar disorder, it may be difficult for family members or doctors to distinguish typical illness behaviors (like severe mood changes in people with

There is a fine line between risky alcohol use and alcohol addiction. A man who drinks more than four drinks a day may be risking his health and safety but is not necessarily addicted to alcohol.

bipolar disorder) from those that may signify addiction. This is especially true since many addicts also have other mental disorders. In 2014, according to SAMHSA, of the 20.2 million American adults with substance addictions, 7.9 million had both a substance addiction and another serious mental illness.

The latest criteria for diagnosing addiction are spelled out in the newest edition of the *Diagnostic and Statistical Manual of Mental Disorders* (DSM-5), which psychiatrists use to diagnose all types of mental illnesses. In the previous DSM, substance dependence and abuse were considered to be separate disorders, but the DSM-5 considers both to represent the same condition. DSM-5 also includes new diagnostic criteria and categories, with the two main addiction categories listed as substance use disorders and gambling disorder. DSM-5 also refers to different types of substance addictions by different names; for instance, it calls alcohol addiction "alcohol use disorder" and stimulant drug addiction "stimulant use disorder."

In order for a patient to qualify as an addict, two or more listed criteria must be present within a twelve-month period. The criteria include spending much time using certain substances or engaging in certain behaviors, hazardous use, and social and interpersonal problems related to the behavior. Other behaviors that make up the criteria for addiction include neglecting important responsibilities, developing tolerance, using increasing amounts of a substance, engaging in repeated attempts to quit or control use, and physical and/or psychological problems related to use.

Not all behaviors that are associated with compulsions are officially categorized as addictions. Eating disorders like anorexia nervosa, for instance, involve compulsions and other qualities that are very similar to those in diagnosable addictions. Yet psychiatrists do not officially consider eating disorders to be addictions. This can

> **WORDS IN CONTEXT**
>
> **tolerance**
> A state that occurs when an addict's body becomes used to a particular substance or behavior, so increasing amounts are needed to achieve the same high, or good feeling.

The Brain and Addiction

Numerous processes in the brain are involved in addiction. The human brain consists of 80 billion to 100 billion neurons (nerve cells) supported by about 1 trillion glial cells. These cells are grouped into brain circuits and systems. The main parts of a neuron are the cell body, axons, and dendrites. The genetic material contained in the cell body directs its activities. Axons are long extensions that transmit electrical signals and chemical messengers called neurotransmitters to other neurons, and dendrites are short extensions that receive neurotransmitters through specific receptors. Different types of neurons release and take up different neurotransmitters, such as dopamine, serotonin, glutamate, and others. These chemicals travel across tiny gaps between neurons called synapses. Once neurotransmitters act on neighboring neurons, the sending neuron recycles them through the reuptake process, in which the neuron reabsorbs and reuses the chemical.

The brain changes related to addiction mostly occur in the cerebral cortex, which governs higher-level thinking and decision making, and the limbic system, which coordinates memory, emotions, and goal-seeking behavior. These changes involve altered neurotransmitter levels and neuron firing rates, along with neuron growth and death and changes in the number, shape, and growth of synapses.

Substances and behaviors involved in addiction create and are also affected by these changes in synapses and neurotransmitters, particularly the neurotransmitter dopamine, which underlies feelings of euphoria. Cocaine, for instance, prevents dopamine reuptake and thus increases dopamine levels by leaving it in synapses for longer than normal. In contrast, nicotine stimulates neurons to release more dopamine than normal.

create confusion among the public and indeed among doctors in some cases, especially since many doctors consider compulsive food intake that leads to extreme obesity to be a form of addiction.

Is Addiction a Disease?

There is also much debate about what addiction is—whether it constitutes a disease, a habit, or a moral deficiency. Throughout much of history, social and cultural stigmas hindered efforts to understand the nature of addiction, and these stigmas still exist to a lesser degree today. As Dr. Nora D. Volkow of NIDA explains, "When scientists began to study addictive behavior in the 1930s, people addicted to drugs were thought to be morally flawed and lacking in willpower. Those views shaped society's responses to drug abuse, treating it as a moral failing rather than a health problem, which led to an emphasis on punishment rather than prevention and treatment."[8]

The pendulum has swung in the other direction in the twenty-first century, and many experts (including the American Medical Association and the American Society of Addiction Medicine) believe addiction is a chronic (long-term) brain disease that involves disruptions in areas responsible for reward, judgment, and motivation. "Addiction is a lot like other diseases, such as heart disease. Both disrupt the normal, healthy functioning of the underlying organ, have

Many experts believe that addiction is a chronic brain disease that involves disruptions in areas responsible for reward, judgment, and motivation.

serious harmful consequences, and are preventable and treatable, but if left untreated, can last a lifetime,"[9] explains NIDA.

The disease theory stems in large part from the trend in modern psychiatry to view all mental abnormalities as diseases rather than as manifestations of personal weakness or immorality. Proponents argue that stating that addicts merely suffer from a disease comparable to cancer removes much of the stigma and frees addicts from direct responsibility for making poor choices. In turn, this may make them more amenable to seeking treatment.

Psychiatrist David Sack, an authority on addiction, believes that several factors make addiction a disease. First of all, it is chronic, or long term, and involves frequent relapses, or recurrences, just like many other diseases. Secondly, people who are addicted to one thing are prone to becoming addicted to other things, just like people with autoimmune disorders are prone to developing multiple similar conditions. Thirdly, all types of addicts share similar behavior changes, which suggests that different addictions are actually subtypes of one underlying disease. Fourthly, the fact that certain medications can treat addiction, just like they can treat other chronic diseases, also supports the disease argument.

Studies also support the contention that addiction is similar to other chronic diseases. For example, researchers have discovered that more than 80 percent of heroin addicts relapse within one year after recovering in a treatment program, and more than 90 percent relapse after three years, no matter what sort of treatment they receive. "These outcomes are not dissimilar to those observed in type II diabetes, hypertension, or asthma, where only a minority of patients achieve clinical control after extensive treatment,"[10] Sack writes.

Other experts note that since numerous brain changes underlie addiction, this makes it a disease similar to diseases that affect other body organs. Numerous areas of the brain contribute to addiction. Multiple areas of the cerebral cortex, which governs thinking, learning, problem solving, and other higher brain functions, are involved. So is the limbic system, which sits underneath the cortex and is critical for processing emotions and governing the reward pathways related to feelings of pleasure. As NIDA researchers explain, "Fundamental [brain] processes, when disrupted, can alter voluntary behavioral control, not just in drug addiction but also in other, related disorders of self-regulation, such as obesity and pathological gambling and video-gaming—the so-called behavioral addictions."[11]

Is Addiction a Habit?

Other authorities believe addiction is not a disease but instead stems from personality and learning defects that result in a loss of self-control. Psychologist Stanton Peele is one expert who argues that the brain changes that underlie addiction mainly result from learned responses to addictive substances or behaviors, rather than from a disease process that leads to compulsive behavior. "Addiction is not strictly, or largely, a result of the effects of drugs, even powerful narcotics. Rather, it is determined by the situations of those who use the drugs," Peele states. "The difference between not being addicted and being addicted is the difference between seeing the world as your arena and seeing the world as your prison."[12]

Mental factors like motivation and self-control play a limited role in determining the outcome of diseases like cancer and diabetes. Addiction, Peele and others argue, depends almost entirely on these factors, which makes it a habit rather than a disease. Indeed, studies by University of Michigan neuroscientists Kent Berridge and Terry Robinson found that addiction is governed more by brain connections that control motivation, desire, and impulse than by the brain chemicals that give drug users the euphoria, or high, that leads to physical cravings for the substance.

Other experts point out that many addicts manage to quit drinking, smoking, or pursuing other addictions when the consequences of not quitting become too severe. This is not possible with a disease such as cancer or asthma, for instance. As Columbia University neuroscientist Carl Hart has discovered, giving crack and methamphetamine addicts attractive alternatives to taking these drugs often motivates them to choose the alternatives. For example, many choose to stop using drugs when offered the alternative of money. The well-known Rat Park stud-

Addiction and Love

While addiction is harmful in many ways, it also resembles natural processes that are critical for species survival—love and pair bonding. Indeed, Emory University researchers James Burkett and Larry Young have evidence that addiction constitutes an extreme and harmful extension of the tendency of humans and some animals to fall in love.

The researchers point out that when people fall in love or experience infatuation, they exhibit addiction-like behaviors such as obsessively thinking about and relentlessly pursuing the loved one, even if this disrupts other aspects of their lives. As happens when an addiction ends, the end of a love relationship is also painful and traumatic. And while love creates strong, positive relationships in many cases, its compulsive elements can ruin lives and families. For example, in a well-publicized case in 2009, South Carolina governor Mark Sanford disappeared for six days. He finally admitted that he flew to Argentina to be with a woman he loved, despite the fact that the affair destroyed his reputation and marriage, ruined his relationship with his children, and ended his political career.

Burkett and Young note that the parts of the brain and brain chemicals involved in falling in love and addiction are identical. Both pair bonding and addiction in laboratory rodents and humans involve identical neurotransmitter release patterns and neuron connections in the prefrontal cortex and striatum. The patterns and connections in the prefrontal cortex govern decision making, self-control, and emotional control. Those in the striatum coordinate many cognitive, decision-making, and reward-driven functions in the cortex.

ies conducted by Canadian psychologist Bruce Alexander in the 1970s and 1980s also support this model. In these studies, laboratory rats living in isolation became addicted to and ingested morphine to the point of killing themselves, but changing the environment so it included tasty food, rat companions, and toys led these animals to stop ingesting any addictive drugs because their needs were being otherwise fulfilled.

Brain Changes

Other ammunition for the argument that addiction is not a disease stems from studies that show that the brain changes from any type of learning. "Simply changing the brain doesn't make addiction a disease because not all changes are pathological," writes science journalist and addiction expert Maia Szalavitz. "In order to use brain scans to prove addiction is a disease, you'd have to show changes that are only seen in addicted people, that occur in all cases of addiction and that predict relapse and recovery. No one has done this yet."[13] Indeed, imaging studies indicate that any experiences that are pleasurable or joyful produce the same brain activation and changes in the same areas involved in addiction.

Neuroscientist Marc Lewis, a professor of developmental psychology at Radboud University in the Netherlands, agrees that addiction involves brain changes in what he calls "the neural circuitry of desire," but he notes that the main brain changes are in areas that govern the formation of habits. Addiction, he writes in his book *The Biology of Desire*, is simply "a habit, which like many other habits, gets entrenched through a decrease in self-control."[14] Lewis also notes that other characteristics of addiction, such as personal destructiveness, do not make it a disease either: "The irrationality (including self-destructiveness) of addiction does not indicate that the brain is malfunctioning, as it would if diseased. It just shows that it's a human brain."[15]

Many who reject the disease model find it disturbing for other reasons. For instance, Dr. Peter Grinspoon, who recovered from drug addictions that derailed his medical career for four years, believes the disease label allows addicts to avoid taking responsibility for their actions. As part of his rehabilitation, Grinspoon had to attend a special recovery group for physicians who were recovering from drug, alcohol, gambling, sex, and other addictions. One doctor being treated for sex addiction after engaging in sex with numerous patients especially concerned Grinspoon because Grinspoon believed this man claimed to be afflicted with a disease to avoid accepting personal blame. "I wondered if he was using the guise of 'addict' to get out of trouble with his wife," he writes in his book *Free Refills*. "People shouldn't be allowed to exploit the concept of 'being an addict' to explain any and all types of bad behavior."[16] This issue, like others related to the question of what addiction really is, remains hotly debated as experts struggle to find answers to the problems created by addiction.

CHAPTER 2

What Causes Addiction?

Genetic, biological, emotional, psychological, environmental, and experiential factors all play a role in making certain individuals susceptible to developing addictions and underlie the development of these addictions. Different theories of addiction emphasize different causal elements as being of primary importance. For example, experts who believe addiction is a brain disease emphasize that certain brain changes primarily cause and influence the course of the disease, while those who believe addiction is mostly a destructive habit emphasize the social learning and personal choice factors. However, proponents of these different models agree that complex interactions between biological, environmental, social, and personality factors play a role in causing addiction.

Genetic Contributors to Addiction

The fact that addictions tend to run in families means that genetic factors contribute to their development. However, having the gene mutations (abnormalities) that influence an individual's vulnerability to addiction does not guarantee that the individual will become an addict, nor does it mean that the children of parents with addictions will become addicts. Numerous studies have found that genetic factors account for 40 percent to 60 percent of an individual's addiction risk; this means that other factors like personality, environment, and learning also play a role.

Researchers believe that no single gene is responsible for increasing the risk of addiction. Instead, five to eleven gene mutations most commonly increase an individual's vulnerability. These mutations are in genes that influence how the brain processes neurotransmitters—the chemicals that help neurons communicate. In particular, genes that govern the neurotransmitters dopamine, glutamate, gamma-aminobutyric acid (GABA), and endorphin activity in areas of the brain that regulate reward, pleasure, and self-control are involved. When people engage in potentially addictive pastimes like gambling or taking drugs that affect the brain, those with these gene mutations respond differently to the excessive amounts of dopamine or other neurotransmitters that these activities generate. For example, while the brains of people without a genetic predisposition to addiction counterbalance excess dopamine with other neurotransmitters, the brains of those prone to addiction fail to do this. The result is that addiction-prone individuals cannot control the compulsion to keep repeating the pleasurable experience provided by the extra dopamine.

> **WORDS IN CONTEXT**
>
> ---
>
> **genes**
> The parts of DNA molecules that transmit hereditary information from parents to their offspring.

Studies indicate that some gene mutations that increase the risk of addiction act by limiting the number of dopamine receptors—structures on neuron dendrites that take up dopamine—in brain areas associated with reward and pleasure. This happens both before and after an addiction develops. Having too few dopamine receptors means that affected individuals cannot use much of the dopamine produced in the brain, and this motivates these individuals to engage in activities that produce the extra dopamine they need to feel good. It also drives the ongoing compulsions to keep repeating these behaviors. In the case of food addictions that lead to obesity, "low brain . . . [dopamine] activity in obese subjects predisposes them to excessive use of food,"[17] note researchers at Brookhaven National Laboratory who have studied this issue extensively. Indeed, these researchers discovered that the more obese an individual is, the fewer dopamine receptors he or she has in brain areas that mediate pleasure and habitual behaviors.

Another genetically determined factor that influences addiction is gender. Women are known to become addicted to most addictive substances much faster than men, in part because they tend to be smaller and the substance ends up being more concentrated in a woman's body. Another reason is that there are gender differences in genes that regulate how substances in drugs are broken down in the body. In one study conducted by

Women are known to become addicted to substances much faster than men are, in part because they tend to be smaller, which makes the substance more concentrated in the body.

researchers at Harvard University and other institutions, twelve-to thirteen-year-old girls who began smoking cigarettes became addicted in about 21 days, versus 183 days for boys. Other studies indicate that females become addicted faster to alcohol, cocaine, heroin, and marijuana than males do.

Genetic factors that influence personality also play a role in predisposing people to addiction. Many experts believe people

Brain Areas That Control Addiction Phases

Research by neuroscientist Trevor W. Robbins and his associates at Cambridge University reveals that different brain circuits are responsible for the pleasure-seeking and compulsive-use phases of drug addiction. "The switch from controlled to compulsive drug seeking represents a transition at the neural level from prefrontal cortex to striatal control over drug-seeking and drug-taking behavior," note the researchers.

The prefrontal area of the cerebral cortex plays a big role in governing decision making, self-control, and emotions, while the striatum sits under the cortex in the area known as the basal ganglia and coordinates many of the cognitive, decision-making, and reward-driven functions that occur in the cortex. Both main parts of the striatum, the ventral and dorsal areas, are important in addiction. Part of the ventral striatum, called the nucleus accumbens, is primarily involved in coordinating cortical functions that depend on motivation and reward pathways, while the dorsal striatum mainly coordinates habitual and automatic behaviors associated with certain environmental cues.

Initially, high levels of dopamine in the prefrontal cortex lead to the high that motivates an individual to use a particular substance or to repeat a particular behavior. But gradually, increased dopamine levels in the dorsal striatum underlie the transition to the compulsive behavior that characterizes addiction. However, Robbins and his colleagues found that these processes only occur in rats and humans with a genetic predisposition to addictive behavior. This helps explain why some people who ingest certain drugs or engage in certain behaviors become addicted.

Trevor W. Robbins and Barry J. Everitt, eds., *The Neurobiology of Addiction*. Oxford: Oxford University Press, 2010, p. 38.

born with personality traits known collectively as an addictive personality are especially vulnerable. These traits include being impulsive (acting without thinking things through), aggressive, and drawn to thrill-seeking activities such as hang gliding and base jumping. People prone to addiction also tend to need constant reassurance and comfort from others; in other words, they do not develop the ability to self-regulate their emotions and feelings of worthiness. Addiction experts believe all these inborn behavioral tendencies predispose people to develop the lack of self-control that characterizes addiction.

People with mental disorders like schizophrenia and bipolar disorder are also at increased risk for addiction. In turn, the risk of developing these diseases is heavily influenced by genes.

Environment and Experience

Without the presence of certain environmental conditions and experiences, people with a genetic predisposition for addiction are unlikely to become addicts. An individual's environment at any age can influence his or her vulnerability, but childhood experiences are the most powerful in this regard. In fact, the environment that exists before a baby is born, as well as after birth, has been proved to affect brain development and to have a profound effect on lifelong habits and behavior. For example, babies born to mothers who are depressed or stressed during pregnancy are exposed to large amounts of the stress hormone cortisol, which can reduce the number of dopamine and opioid receptors in parts of the brain that influence later tendencies to addiction.

> **WORDS IN CONTEXT**
>
> **predisposition**
> A tendency to develop a disease or behavior.

Environmental factors that commonly contribute to addiction after birth include poverty; physical, sexual, and emotional abuse; substance addictions in family members or friends; and easy access to addictive substances. The fact that children who grow up in impoverished or violent homes and who lack parental supervision are at much higher risk of addiction than others has been widely studied. Scientists know that these experiences directly affect development and function in areas of the brain involved in emotions, motivation, and self-control. This mostly happens because these experiences affect the growth and survival of neurons, glia, axons, dendrites, and the synapses that govern neural communications.

Many experts believe that environmental effects on brain development during childhood influence later tendencies to develop addiction even more than genes do. This view is supported by a a study of more than seventeen thousand patients with various addictions at the Kaiser Permanente San Diego Medical Center. The researchers found that children exposed to physical, emotional, or sexual abuse; an alcoholic parent; or a depressed parent had a 500 percent increased risk of developing alcoholism and a 4,600 percent increased risk of abusing illegal intravenous

Children who grow up in violent homes with parental conflict are at higher risk of addiction than children raised in supportive environments. This chaos directly affects the development of areas of the brain that regulate self-control, emotions, and motivation.

drugs as adults. This study, known as the Adverse Childhood Experiences Study, began in 1995 and is ongoing. It has also spawned similar studies worldwide.

Other research indicates that environmental events before and after birth can even cause permanent changes in how genes that regulate brain function operate. As science writer Ronald Kotulak explains, "Stress and drugs like cocaine . . . can produce biochemical changes that directly affect the function of some key brain-cell genes, in effect laying down permanent, maladaptive [harmful] behavior patterns."[18] The science of how experiences affect gene expression is called epigenetics, and studies indicate that epigenetic changes can be transmitted from parents to their offspring. Studies by researchers at the University of California–San Francisco, for instance, found that long-term alcohol addiction changes chemicals around certain genes that protect people from addiction. These epigenetic changes in turn raise the risk of addiction in alcoholics' offspring.

Early Drug Use

Another factor that strongly influences the development of addiction is starting to use addictive substances in childhood or adolescence. This happens because the effects of these substances on the developing brain are especially profound and long lasting. Studies show that the earlier an individual starts using addictive drugs, the greater is the risk of future addictions.

Scientists find that people who start using illicit drugs or abusing prescription drugs or alcohol during adolescence have a very high risk of lifetime addiction because these drugs damage the prefrontal cortex, which governs decision making, self-control, and emotional control. This area undergoes significant development during adolescence, and the brain damage that results from certain drugs like alcohol and cocaine is thus especially likely to affect these mental capabilities.

In addition, early drug use often coincides with other risk factors, such as living in an unstable family in which family members have mental illnesses and children are unsupervised or abused. The cumulative effect of these risk factors makes it even more

likely that a given individual will become addicted to substances and/or behaviors.

Even when early drug use does not coexist with risk factors like abuse, it is still a powerful determinant of later addiction. Peter Grinspoon, a respected physician who became addicted to prescription pain medications, grew up in a prosperous, loving home (his father was a noted psychiatrist), but his politically liberal parents openly used marijuana and other illegal drugs with colleagues and friends. Although the parents hid their drugs from their children, the kids knew exactly where to find them, and Peter began smoking pot regularly while in junior high school and continued in high school, college, and beyond. Because of his parents' attitudes, he thought marijuana and other illegal drugs were harmless, and he also developed an acceptance of doing (and hiding) illegal things.

Complex Interactions

However, having numerous risk factors for addiction does not necessarily mean an individual will become an addict. Lacy's childhood in Minnesota, for instance, included having an alcoholic mother who physically and verbally abused her and living with her mother in homes of various alcoholic, abusive men. Although Lacy had ample genetic and environmental risk factors for addiction, she somehow found the strength to overcome the depression, fear, and helplessness she felt and to resist addictive substances. As a teen, she left her mother and founded a support group for children of alcoholics. "The darkest moments of my life sparked a passion in me that cannot be put out,"[19] she writes.

Conversely, growing up in a supportive, loving home does not guarantee that an individual will not become an addict. Both Sandy and Peter grew up in loving, well-to-do suburban homes in New Jersey, but both became heroin addicts while dealing with the stresses involved in raising their four children. Clearly, complex interactions between biological, personality, environmental, and learning factors contribute to causing addiction.

Stress, Change, and Addiction

Although early experiences are important for triggering addiction, stressful life events like divorce, death of a loved one, severe illness, or losing one's job can all precipitate addiction in genetically susceptible people at any time. Indeed, researchers find that anyone undergoing stressful life changes is more susceptible to addiction. This again is one reason why adolescents are at increased risk for addiction—this phase of life is fraught with the physical and emotional changes that accompany the transition from childhood to adulthood. In addition, teenagers are concerned with fitting into social groups of their peers, and when friends are experimenting with drugs and alcohol, it can be difficult to say no.

In fact, most addictions begin as methods of helping people feel better and cope with unpleasant experiences or to fit in with peers. For some, the pain they seek to initially escape is emotional. For others, an addiction to painkillers and similar drugs starts when the individual is legitimately given these medications for physical pain from an accident, surgery, or other medical problem. But addiction-prone people continue to take the drug after the physical need vanishes, because the drug makes them feel relaxed or high. This is because drugs intended to treat physical pain act on the same brain centers that govern emotional pain. These areas interpret physical and emotional pain in similar ways, and it is very easy for biologically susceptible people to become unable to distinguish the difference. As Canadian physician and addiction expert Gabor Maté explains in his book *In the Realm of Hungry Ghosts*, "The very same brain centers that interpret and feel physical pain also become activated during the experience of emotional rejection: on brain scans they 'light up' in response to social ostracism just as they would when triggered by physically harmful stimuli."[20]

What Results from Brain Changes

Although interactions between social, psychological, emotional, and biological factors determine the risk of addiction, the actual direct cause is the brain changes that result from these interactions. These changes primarily occur in the striatum and the prefrontal cortex.

Although these brain changes can be characterized as either a disease or a dangerous learned habit, they occur through normal processes that utilize neuroplasticity. This is the ability of the brain to change in response to learning or experience. For example, pleasurable activities like eating good food or falling in love activate dopamine circuits just as drugs like cocaine do, and an individual may learn to keep repeating the activity to achieve the pleasurable feeling.

WORDS IN CONTEXT

neuroplasticity
The ability of the brain to change in response to experiences or learning.

Addiction Is Caused by Human Factors

Many people mistakenly believe that certain "addictive" drugs cause addiction. For instance, many who are addicted to opiate painkillers state that a doctor caused the addiction by prescribing these drugs for postsurgical pain. However, as Harvard University psychiatrist Lance Dodes explains, "Addiction is a human problem that resides in people, not in the drug or in the drug's capacity to produce physical effects." Indeed, many people take prescription pain medicines without becoming addicted, because the drugs themselves do not cause addiction. Instead, those who become addicted already have genetic, environmental, experiential, biological, and/or other risk factors that predispose them to addiction.

The same is true of other types of addiction. All people who ingest food certainly do not become compulsive eaters, nor does everyone who gambles become addicted to gambling. The fact that many addicts have multiple addictions also stems from the fact that people actually become addicted to their own brain chemistry, and any of a number of substances or behaviors can fuel this process. A study of over seventeen thousand Americans enrolled in weight-loss programs at the Kaiser Permanente San Diego Medical Center supports this contention; many obese patients were also addicted to alcohol, cigarettes, and illegal drugs.

Some doctors and drug policy experts find these facts disturbing because they place responsibility for addiction on addicts' genes, environment, and learned behaviors rather than attaching blame to the drugs themselves. Others view these facts as important tools for helping addicts understand how they can overcome their addictions.

Lance Dodes, *The Heart of Addiction*. New York: HarperCollins, 2002, p. 73.

When a behavior like this is under an individual's conscious control, it is primarily governed by the prefrontal cortex. But when an addiction takes hold, control shifts to the striatum, and the behavior becomes compulsive. When this happens, the brain loses its ability to regulate and respond to natural dopamine release, and the addicted person depends on external sources of dopamine to feel pleasure.

Over time, these brain changes lead to tolerance and cravings. Positron emission tomography imaging studies on rhesus monkeys conducted by Dr. Michael Nader and his colleagues at Wake Forest University help explain how this happens. These studies show that the longer the monkeys used cocaine, the more the number of dopamine receptors in the basal ganglia (the area in which the striatum sits) decreased. This meant that the animals needed more cocaine to achieve the same effects the longer they used the drug. The studies also found that monkeys that developed cocaine addiction in the first place had fewer-than-normal dopamine receptors in the prefrontal cortex and striatum. Thus, it appears that having too few dopamine receptors plays a role in making individuals vulnerable to developing addictions and that prolonged use of drugs further reduces these numbers. This thereby affects addicts' ability to make decisions and underlies their diminished responsiveness to addictive substances.

Nader and other researchers have also demonstrated that the number of dopamine receptors in these brain areas can increase after an animal or person stops using a particular drug, but the rate of increase depends on the individual. In some people and animals, for example, the number of receptors increases after one month, while in others it takes a year. "Understanding how long-term cocaine exposure affects dopamine receptor function could ultimately lead to better treatment strategies,"[21] the researchers note, especially since further knowledge can shed light on the biochemical differences that make certain addicts more or less likely to develop more dopamine receptors over time.

This type of biological and behavioral research has enhanced experts' understanding of the diverse causes of addiction. Even so, the 2016 US surgeon general's report on addiction points out that much more research, particularly research that explores the biological underpinnings, is still needed. "Continued research is necessary to more thoroughly explain how substance use affects the brain at the molecular, cellular, and circuit levels,"[22] the report states. Studies that seek to better understand these mechanisms and their interactions with psychological, environmental, and social causes of different types of addiction are therefore under way.

CHAPTER 3

Prevention of Addiction

The key to preventing addiction, many public health officials and educators have come to believe, lies not in moralizing about human frailties or enacting stiffer punishments but in developing strategies based on the social, biological, and emotional causes of addiction. Most current efforts are therefore directed at reducing known risk factors and strengthening protective factors. Different communities have launched different programs that seek to improve school and home environments so they include more of these protective factors.

Risk Factors and Protective Factors

The factors that contribute to addiction are many and varied. Major risk factors for addiction include peer pressure, childhood trauma, stress, and early drug use. Factors that may help protect people from addiction are growing up with loving, attentive, supportive parents; learning to behave responsibly and exercising self-control; not using drugs during adolescence; and striving to do well in school, sports, and other positive activities. Being educated in schools that foster academic excellence, teach students about drug abuse, and have strict anti-drug policies is also a protective factor. Furthermore, growing up in a safe neighborhood with positive role models and productive, helpful neighbors has also been proved to help protect people from addiction.

Researchers have determined that the most powerful protective factor is preventing the early use of addictive substances. "When addicts entering addiction treatment are asked when they

A key factor that can protect people from addiction is growing up with loving and supportive parents. Children who grow up in negative environments are more likely to abuse substances.

first began drinking or using drugs, the answer is almost always the same: They started when they were young teenagers,"[23] states Dr. John Knight of the Center for Adolescent Substance Abuse Research at Boston Children's Hospital. Studies conducted by SAMHSA confirm that the majority of illicit drug use begins anywhere between the ages of twelve and twenty, and according to NIDA, "if we can prevent young people from experimenting with drugs, we can prevent addiction."[24]

Preventing Early Illicit Drug Use

Other studies prove that delaying the use of substances like tobacco and alcohol while the brain is still developing during adolescence significantly reduces the risk of later substance abuse and addiction. For example, studies show that 25 percent of Americans who started using an addictive substance before age eighteen are addicted, whereas 4 percent of those who started using such substances at age twenty-one or older are addicted. Based

Preventing Drug Abuse and Addiction in Iceland

Teens in Iceland had one of the highest alcohol-consumption rates in Europe in the 1990s. "There were hordes of teenagers getting in-your-face drunk," says American psychologist Harvey Milkman, who teaches at Reykjavik University.

Milkman helped the Icelandic government design the Youth in Iceland program to prevent alcohol and drug use in adolescents. The program is based on his research in the 1970s that led him to conclude that people become addicted to changes in their own brain chemistry and that participating regularly in organized sports and wholesome family activities gives teens the high they want without alcohol and drugs. The government initiated regular survey taking in schools to determine what kids wanted and built facilities like an indoor skating rink, swimming pool, badminton courts, and more to satisfy teens' needs for positive places to hang out. Schools began music, art, dance, and other clubs, and laws were enacted that prohibited teens from buying tobacco and alcohol and required parents to sign agreements in which they promised to prohibit alcohol at teen parties.

The results continue to impress residents and outsiders; in fact, many localities have based similar preventive programs on the Icelandic model. In 1998, 42 percent of the fifteen- and sixteen-year-olds in Iceland admitted that they had been drunk in the previous month, 17 percent had used marijuana, and 23 percent smoked cigarettes. In 2016, only 5 percent had been drunk in the previous month, 7 percent had used marijuana, and 3 percent had smoked cigarettes.

Quoted in Emma Young, "How Iceland Got Teens to Say No to Drugs," *Atlantic*, January 19, 2017. www.the atlantic.com.

on these findings and on related studies, numerous communities have made the prevention of adolescent drug use a priority.

One method aimed at reducing early drug use involves controlling adolescents' access to these substances. Many localities have raised taxes on tobacco and alcohol products, with the goal of making them unaffordable for the average teenager. Another common method of restricting access is to require store owners to keep these products behind sales counters or in other places that require store employees to remove them before someone purchases them. Many places have also strengthened punishments for adults who buy these products for minors and for mi-

One method aimed at reducing early drug use is controlling adolescents' access to tobacco and alcohol by requiring store owners to keep these products behind sales counters or in another restricted area.

nors who use fraudulent driver's licenses to buy them illegally. Laws also prohibit manufacturers from advertising and marketing these products in ways that target young people.

A variety of education programs in schools also seek to reinforce antidrug messages. One long-term preventive program known as Drug Abuse Resistance Education (D.A.R.E.) has received mixed reviews but is used in 75 percent of US school districts and in forty-three countries. D.A.R.E. was introduced in the United States in 1983 as a classroom-based antidrug educational program taught by local police officers. Some studies indicate that D.A.R.E. is counterproductive and may actually increase drug use among young people. However, many students, teachers, and law enforcement agencies praise its effectiveness in raising awareness of drug-related issues and in improving relations between students and police officers. In general, though, the original D.A.R.E. program is considered to be largely ineffective in preventing drug use and abuse.

In contrast, the newer keepin' it REAL D.A.R.E. program for middle school students, which was introduced in 2009, has been widely acclaimed for its effectiveness. A 2014 *Scientific American* article explains that keepin' it REAL replaces "long, drug-fact laden lectures with interactive lessons that present stories meant to help kids make smart decisions."[25] In 2016 the US surgeon general issued a report stating that keepin' it REAL had lowered drug use in many communities. The program was developed by Pennsylvania State University professors on the basis of input from adolescents. It engages students in acting out role-playing scenarios to help them develop decision-making strategies that include the *Refuse*, *Explain*, *Avoid*, and *Leave* elements of the acronym *REAL*. "What I learned from keepin it REAL is that when it comes to drugs and alcohol, just think, 'No!'" says middle school student Maria Andrews. "Leaving is one of the easiest things to do. You don't need any explanations or excuses."[26]

True-Life Lessons

Besides using these well-known D.A.R.E. programs, many schools sponsor talks by law enforcement personnel, medical experts, and former addicts to give students firsthand insight into the world of drug addiction. These personal-experience presentations are proving to be more effective than simply telling children and adolescents about the bad things addictions do. Interacting with former addicts is especially effective in motivating students to avoid drug use.

Many former addicts devote their spare time and/or become professional addiction counselors and educators to help in this way. Former NBA player Chris Herren, whose addiction to alcohol, cocaine, heroin, OxyContin, and other drugs cost him his basketball career, is an example of someone who is trying to prevent addiction in young people. He founded the nonprofit Herren Project to help educate students about why addiction prevention is so important and to help addicts pay for treatment. Herren gives about 250 school presentations each year. His talks inspire and empower thousands of students to resist peer pressure and to ask for help if they are struggling with drug problems or self-esteem issues that commonly trigger drug addiction and overdoses. Rather than focusing on the story of his recovery like most former addicts do, Herren shares details about what triggered his drug use and how it evolved into the compulsive behaviors that ruined his life. He finds this approach to be more productive because it reinforces preventive efforts. "We need to focus on the first day rather than on the worst day . . . on where [addiction] begins rather than where it ends,"[27] he states.

In a similar manner, school-based programs that demonstrate the real-world consequences of addiction tend to have an effect on youth. Programs that highlight the dangers of nicotine addiction often involve medical practitioners showing students black-coated lungs removed from deceased smokers or bringing in longtime smokers who have undergone a tracheostomy so that they can breathe. In a tracheostomy, a surgeon cuts a hole in the windpipe and the neck and a tube is inserted through those holes to allow air into the lungs. In fact, studies by researchers at the University of Michigan have shown that cigarette smoking among teens has diminished since these types of education programs were initiated in the mid-1970s. On the other hand, marijuana use among teens has increased since 1991, when US states started legalizing the drug for medical use. Programs presented by police officers and paramedics, which show students videos of traffic accidents caused by drunk or high drivers, also tend to be effective in discouraging these behaviors.

Despite the success of these programs, addiction experts acknowledge that there is still much work to do. As revealed in SAMHSA's latest report, published in 2014, about 2.2 million American adolescents used illegal drugs that year. And many of those individuals are likely to develop addictions.

Screenings

Other prevention programs emphasize screening children and teenagers to identify risk factors that raise their risk of addiction and taking steps to reduce those risk factors. Many such programs are new, but preliminary assessments indicate that some are effective. The Preventure program, for instance, uses personality tests administered in schools or community centers to identify at-risk kids. The personality traits linked to addiction that raise red flags are sensation seeking, compulsiveness, hopelessness, and anxiety sensitivity, and numerous localities are implementing counseling intervention programs for children with these traits. Early evaluations indicate that Preventure screenings can identify 90 percent of high-risk children.

Other prevention efforts focus on screening teens for substance abuse during routine doctor's office checkups. Such screenings may include oral and written questionnaires, clinicians' observations, and laboratory tests that detect drugs in blood, urine, saliva, or hair samples. These programs are part of larger efforts to bring addiction prevention and treatment into the realm of mainstream medical practice, since most addiction clinics are run by nonmedical professionals such as licensed or unlicensed counselors. Few medical doctors perform routine addiction screenings, and many addiction experts believe doing so would enhance prevention efforts.

A 2016 US surgeon general's report also noted that bringing addiction screenings and treatment into mainstream health care systems would go a long way toward reducing the associated stigma. As the report explained, the common view of addiction as a personal failing rather than a medical issue has been reinforced by the fact that most addiction care and prevention programs have been administered outside the medical world. It noted "With the exception of detoxification in hospital-based settings, virtually all treatment was delivered by programs that were geographically, financially, culturally, and organizationally separate from mainstream health care."[28] It also noted that laws that require medical insurance companies to cover addiction care are among the factors that are gradually shifting addiction programs to health care clinics.

Preventive Interventions

Although most screening and intervention programs are still outside mainstream medicine, some have proved effective in preventing drug addiction. One such program is called Screening, Brief Intervention, and Referral to Treatment. Under this program, social workers visit schools and public health centers to administer screening questionnaires and observe students and patients. Based on personal observations and questionnaire results, social workers or addiction counselors then visit the homes of at-risk children and teens or invite them to community counseling centers for brief educational interventions. The interventions may involve giving advice about how to resist peer pressure or how to contact law enforcement agencies about substance abuse in the home. When social workers believe further interventions are needed, teens are referred to extended counseling programs. The short- and long-term interventions often employ a technique called motivational interviewing, which "is about guiding someone to make a healthy choice, versus saying, 'Okay, you have a problem and you need to change,'"[29] explains clinical psychologist Elizabeth D'Amico.

In some cases social workers speak with parents and other caregivers about the importance of having strict antidrug rules at home and about how adults' behaviors influence children's choices. For

Recoding Memories to Prevent Addiction

Some scientists believe it may someday be possible to prevent drug addiction from occurring or from returning in recovering addicts by manipulating memories. Researchers have known for many years that using drugs like cocaine produces long-lasting changes, or memory traces called engrams, in neurons in the amygdala (part of the limbic system that is important in memory formation and emotions). Backup copies of these engrams form in specialized neurons called place cells in the nearby hippocampus. Place cells become active when a person or animal enters the environment in which the memory was encoded. Thus, the neural activation patterns in place cells represent a cognitive map that identifies where the memory was made. In turn, place cell activation often triggers cravings for the drug associated with the engram.

In 2016 researchers led by Stephanie Trouche at the University of Oxford discovered that they could recode engrams in place cells in drug-addicted mice. They used a technique called optigenetics. Optigenetics involves activating light-sensitive proteins in the brain. Recoding an engram erased the memory of the environmental cues associated with the drug use and prevented drug cravings in these mice.

These researchers believe this technique might someday be used to prevent drug addiction or relapse triggered by environmental cues. However, bioethicists (people who study the ethics of biomedicine) have already raised concerns about the morality of manipulating memories in humans. Such concerns may limit the use of such techniques if they become viable.

example, parents who abuse alcohol or prescription drugs might not realize how their behavior influences their children. Children often follow the examples—both good and bad—set by parents.

Lessons from Vietnam

Other preventive strategies evolved out of studies of soldiers who served in the Vietnam War in the 1960s and 1970s. In 1971 several members of Congress visited American soldiers in Vietnam and found that about 15 percent were addicted to heroin. The public was appalled, and President Richard Nixon set up the Special Action Office for Drug Abuse Prevention to fight and prevent these types of addictions. Nixon also commissioned psychiatric researcher Lee Robins and her colleagues to track the soldiers' progress once they returned to the United States. Before coming home, the soldiers received therapy to help them recover.

To everyone's surprise, 95 percent of the soldiers did not use heroin again once they were back in the United States. This was surprising because statistics at the time indicated that about 90 percent of drug addicts relapsed and became readdicted after completing therapy. Subsequent research helped explain the soldiers' lack of relapse and also provided insight into viable methods of preventing addiction.

Psychologists discovered that it is extremely difficult for people to change habitual behaviors that are repeated over and over in the same environment, even if they fully intend to do so. The problem is that these behaviors are controlled by environmental cues rather than by conscious intentions. In other words, the behaviors become automatic. For example, each time an individual sits down at his or her kitchen table to eat breakfast, he or she does not think about pulling out the chair, sitting down, picking up the fork, and so on, because the behavior has been repeated so often that it becomes automatic. In a similar manner, if an alcoholic drinks twelve cans of beer while sitting on the couch watching television every night, the behavior becomes automatic and is thus very difficult to change. However, if the environment changes, this disrupts the automatic sequence of events and makes it much easier to defeat a habit. Thus, a therapist might tell an

In 1971 several members of Congress visited troops fighting in the Vietnam War and found that about 15 percent were addicted to heroin. This prompted President Nixon to take action.

alcoholic to move the TV set into a different room and to consciously pour a can of soda into a glass to drink while watching TV, instead of automatically opening and drinking twelve cans of beer. Disrupting the habit makes it much easier for the individual to defeat it if he or she has resolved to do so.

Psychologists determined that the change in environment that occurred when the soldiers returned home from Vietnam helped them stay away from the heroin to which they were addicted in Vietnam. Since then, some efforts to prevent various types of addiction center on altering the environment.

Rat Park and Human Addiction

The Rat Park studies performed by Canadian psychologist Bruce Alexander in the 1970s and 1980s provided further ammunition for addiction prevention and treatment programs that emphasize environmental change. In these studies Alexander placed laboratory rats in isolated living conditions. When he enriched the environment by providing rat companions, tasty food, and toys, he observed that this motivated the rats to give up their addiction to morphine. Indeed, Alexander's research helped scientists prove that environmental and social conditions, rather than inherent properties of drugs themselves, underlie addiction and associated behaviors.

Studies on human addiction by Columbia University neuroscientist Carl Hart built on the Rat Park studies. Hart's work contributed to the development of new methods of preventing and treating drug addictions by changing the environment and social situation of addicts. He discovered that many crack cocaine and methamphetamine addicts who live in impoverished areas stop using these drugs when given attractive incentives, such as money, that improve their life situation. This does not mean that poverty causes addiction; instead, it is one factor that increases the risk because it can contribute to peoples' overall dissatisfaction with life. Thus, this type of prevention program depends on determining what factors lead to the emptiness and dissatisfaction with life that motivate certain people to turn to drugs. In fact, Hart believes the reason so many impoverished people turn to drugs is that they have no other options for enriching or enjoying their lives. "If you're living in a poor neighborhood deprived of options, there's a certain rationality to keep taking a drug that will give you some temporary pleasure," Hart states. "The key factor is the environment, whether you're talking about humans or rats. . . . When you enrich their environment, and give them access to sweets and let them play with other rats, they stop pressing the lever [that administers drugs like cocaine]."[30]

The Future

Despite these advances, addiction experts agree that more research and resources are needed to expand and improve prevention efforts of all types. Some current research focuses on how health care and social service providers, families, educators, and criminal justice administrators can incorporate knowledge about risk factors into preventing addiction. Scientists are also researching biological preventive measures such as addiction vaccines.

Most vaccines are given to prevent infectious diseases like polio or measles. They contain harmless virus parts that stimulate the recipient's immune system to make antibodies (chemicals that attack a particular pathogen). These antibodies will then neutralize the live virus if the recipient is later exposed to it. Vaccines being tested to prevent substance addictions operate in a similar manner. Doctors inject a target addictive drug that is mixed with a protein called a carrier protein. Drug molecules are too small to stimulate an immune response, but carrier proteins are large enough to do so. Then, if the drug is later injected, the antibodies produced in response to the vaccine destroy the drug so it does not enter the brain to make the individual high. Although no drug vaccines have been approved, some are being tested experimentally. For example, Baylor College of Medicine psychiatry professor Thomas Kosten and his colleagues have created and are testing cocaine, nicotine, and methamphetamine vaccines.

Although preliminary studies show that these vaccines work well, Kosten notes that "the primary risk is that a user takes a large amount of the drug to try to override the vaccine. . . . At high doses, some amounts of the drug [escape from] the antibodies."[31] Doctors would thus only administer such vaccines to people who are highly motivated to not become addicted or to not relapse if in recovery.

CHAPTER 4

Treating and Overcoming Addiction

There is no known cure for addiction, but a variety of short- and long-term treatments are being used to help addicts recover and manage the condition. According to NIDA, the main goal of treatment is to enable addicts "to counteract addiction's powerful disruptive effects on their brain and behavior and regain control of their lives."[32] This can be achieved with medical treatments, therapy, and support systems.

Ongoing Deficiencies

Despite the availability of a range of treatment options, numerous factors prevent widespread use of or success with most of these methods. CASA notes that "only about 1 in 10 people with addiction involving alcohol or drugs other than nicotine receive any form of treatment."[33] Many addicts and families report that this is mainly because the associated stigma makes them reluctant to seek treatment. The high costs at most rehabilitation clinics also limit participation. For example, in 2016 the Recovery.org website, which helps addicts navigate the addiction recovery process, reported that inpatient rehabilitation clinics charged from $2,000 to $25,000 per month and that outpatient clinics charged anywhere from nothing to $10,000 per month. Medical insurance rarely covers these costs.

Another issue that pervades addiction treatment is that most addicts relapse. Addiction experts like psychiatrist Akikur Mohammad thus believe major changes in treatment plans are needed. As Mohammad notes in his book *The Anatomy of Addiction*, most addiction rehabilitation clinics in the United States use twelve-step methods modeled on Alcoholics Anonymous, and these programs rarely lead to lasting recovery, even though they claim high success rates. Psychiatrist Lance Dodes, who has studied the effectiveness of these programs, concludes that only 5 percent to 8 percent of twelve-step participants achieve long-term sobriety. This is why many experts believe these programs should be used in conjunction with other therapies rather than by themselves.

But while combining these programs with what Mohammad calls "evidence-based medicine"[34] would decrease relapse rates, this "would greatly increase the cost of doing business and diminish profits if rehab clinics adopted a scientific approach. . . . Evidence-based medicine must be administered by trained medical professionals."[35] Twelve-step programs, in contrast, can be administered by anyone.

According to NIDA, clinicians with specialized training and credentials achieve the best treatment results. Yet studies by CASA

Studies show that clinicians with specialized addiction training and credentials provide the best results with addiction therapy. However, most addiction counselors do not have any medical training.

find that few medical professionals practice addiction therapy. "Addiction counselors, who make up the largest share of providers of addiction treatment services, provide care for patients with a medical disease yet they are not required to have any medical training, and most states do not require them to have any advanced education of any sort,"[36] one study notes.

Choice Versus Powerlessness

The debate over whether addiction is a disease, character weakness, or bad habit is closely tied to debates over how it should be treated. Some experts who believe it is either a moral failing or a disease agree that addicts are powerless to control their cravings and thus need ongoing medical and/or motivational therapy that emphasizes total abstinence from the offending substance or behavior. Others believe that addicts can and do choose to recover and are not slaves to their disease or destructive tendencies. CASA is one prominent organization that takes a middle ground: "People do not choose how their brain and body respond to drugs and alcohol, which is why people with addiction cannot control their use while others can. . . .

[However], people with addiction can still stop using—it's just much harder than it is for someone who has not become addicted."[37]

Some who oppose the disease model believe that viewing addiction as a disease prevents addicts from receiving effective treatment. Neuroscientist Marc Lewis, for example, notes that both the disease model and twelve-step treatment programs make addicts believe that they are stuck with a chronic disease or personal weakness that will never go away. However, he and other former addicts point out that they can and do choose to recover permanently.

Starting Treatment

One thing that authorities agree on is that overcoming addiction is very difficult and that ideal treatment varies according to an indi-

Are Interventions Productive?

Some addiction experts believe interventions are productive methods of motivating addicts to enter and remain in treatment facilities. An intervention is a face-to-face meeting between an addict and people affected by the addict's behavior—usually family members—that is commonly orchestrated by a licensed interventionist. This approach has been popularized by reality television shows such as *Intervention*. *Intervention* features true stories about how interventionists help families stage interventions in which they issue an ultimatum to the addict to either start treatment or risk losing contact and support from loved ones.

Although former addicts and families featured on these shows often tout the positive results, not all experts believe that interventions are productive or effective. "Confrontational approaches in general, though once the norm even in many behavioral treatment settings, have not been found effective and may backfire by heightening resistance and diminishing self-esteem on the part of the targeted individual," states the 2016 US surgeon general's report *Facing Addiction in America*.

In one less-than-successful case, a family staged an intervention facilitated by an interventionist for Elizabeth, a young woman who was addicted to several illegal drugs. The family told Elizabeth how she was hurting them, and her resulting guilt made her halfheartedly agree to enter a rehabilitation clinic. However, a week later she ran away from the clinic because she said the therapists and her family made her feel useless and worthless. She also realized she did not want to be sober. This illustrates the fact that, like other treatment plans, the results of intervention-based programs vary widely.

US Department of Health and Human Services, Office of the Surgeon General, *Facing Addiction in America*. Washington, DC: Health and Human Services, 2016. https://addiction.surgeongeneral.gov.

vidual's specific addictions and needs. Most addicts do best with a variety of treatment elements, which may include a stay at a rehabilitation center, supervised aftercare, support groups, counseling, medication, or other measures. The first step in any type of treatment involves an addict expressing an intense desire and commitment to recover. This desire can be triggered by a variety of events. For Teresa, a longtime drug addict, the event that finally put her on the road to recovery was that her infant said "Mama" for the first time. Prior to that event, Teresa had tried to quit numerous times but always relapsed. She was even unable to quit after the courts labeled her an unfit mother and took her baby away several months before the "Mama" event occurred during a supervised visit. But once Teresa decided she had to quit, she began seeing a therapist and attending recovery meetings.

With substance addictions, the next step in treatment involves detoxifying from the drug, which requires medical assistance and supervision to prevent harmful and possibly fatal withdrawal symptoms such as seizures, vomiting, and delirium. For example, during Peter Grinspoon's withdrawal from his longtime addiction to huge doses of prescription pain pills and tranquilizers, doctors at his rehabilitation facility prescribed three different sedatives—phenobarbital, Neurontin, and Seroquel—to prevent seizures during the withdrawal process. The precise medicines prescribed and the duration of detoxification depend on each individual, but most last ten days to two weeks.

> ### WORDS IN CONTEXT
>
> **delirium**
> A state in which brain function changes rapidly and leads to severe confusion and sometimes to hallucinations and hyperactivity, due to a drug overdose, drug toxicity, or withdrawal from an addictive substance.

Then, medications that mimic or block the effects of the addictive drugs are often used to help addicts stay away from the drugs. For instance, those addicted to nicotine often use nicotine-replacement patches, gum, or pills to help the brain adjust to the lack of nicotine. Alcoholics often use acamprosate, which reduces cravings, or disulfiram, which makes the individual sick if he or she ingests alcohol. Those addicted to opioids often use methadone, buprenorphine, naltrexone, or a combination of buprenorphine and naloxone called Suboxone.

Many recovering addicts use these medications on an ongoing basis—often for the rest of their lives. However, these medications are expensive, and often the government programs that pay for medications for those who cannot afford them have limits. For instance, some state Medicaid programs only pay for Suboxone

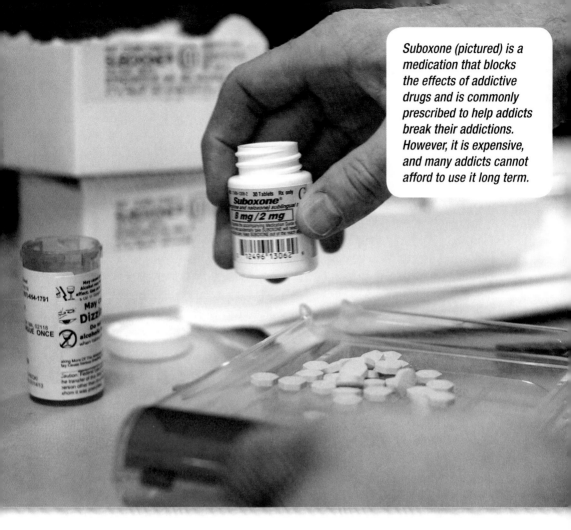

Suboxone (pictured) is a medication that blocks the effects of addictive drugs and is commonly prescribed to help addicts break their addictions. However, it is expensive, and many addicts cannot afford to use it long term.

for three years. This can disrupt treatment and often leads to re-lapses in people who cannot pay for these medications.

It can also be difficult to find a doctor to prescribe drugs like Suboxone. As part of efforts to control the prescription painkiller abuse epidemic, in 2013 the CDC and the Drug Enforcement Administration forbade doctors other than those who are specially certified from prescribing narcotic painkillers and addiction treatment drugs. This has led many former prescription drug addicts to switch to widely available (and illegal) heroin and also to sell Suboxone illegally.

Recovery Versus Sobriety

Medical treatment with antiaddiction drugs rarely has lasting effects unless it is combined with therapy. Without psychological

Recovery in the Brain

Before the 1950s scientists believed that abnormal brain development that increased the risk of addiction in traumatized children could not be reversed. However, researchers have determined that some of the damage can be undone when addicts undergo cognitive behavioral therapy and stop using drugs. Three main types of research led to these findings. First, in the 1950s neuroscientist Marian Diamond proved that sensory enrichment at any phase of life leads to brain growth and enhances brain connections. More recent studies on obsessive-compulsive disorder, which is similar to addiction, were done by Dr. Jeffrey M. Schwartz at the University of California–Los Angeles. Schwartz found that people with obsessive-compulsive disorder can learn to change their thoughts and behaviors in order to replace deeply ingrained brain circuits that underlie their compulsions. As Schwartz explains, "The brain remodels itself throughout life. . . . It retains the capacity to change itself as the result not only of passively experienced factors, such as enriched environments, but also of changes in the ways we behave and the ways we think."

In addition, researchers led by psychiatrist Colm G. Connolly of the University of California–San Francisco discovered that brain areas that shrink in long-term cocaine addicts can recover some of their cognitive and decision-making functions if the addict stops taking the drug. However, the researchers noted, "recovery is not simply a reversal of the process of disease." Instead, other areas of the brain take over the functions that were impaired by the brain damage.

Jeffrey M. Schwartz and Sharon Begley, *The Mind and the Brain.* New York: HarperCollins, 2002, pp. 253–54.

Colm G. Connolly et al., "Dissociated Grey Matter Changes with Prolonged Addiction and Extended Abstinence in Cocaine Users," *PLoS ONE*, March 18, 2013, p. e59645.

counseling, many addicts who manage to overcome one addiction simply take on a new addiction to serve the self-soothing function their addictions fulfill. Anne, for example, recovered from her addiction to alcohol. However, she did not participate in therapy to help her understand that she routinely coped with life's realities by using activities that increased her dopamine levels. She immediately developed a food addiction that made her gain an enormous amount of weight. As physician and addiction expert Gabor Maté explains, addicts who only change one behavior without changing their underlying coping style merely abstain from one behavior without achieving sobriety, which is a more lasting accomplishment. "In choosing sobriety we're not so much avoiding something harmful as envisioning ourselves living the life we value,"[38] he writes. Indeed, sobriety involves finding positive methods of fulfilling one's needs rather than simply abandoning an addiction.

Lewis notes that making a conscious effort to change one's situation makes it possible to learn new habits. With time, those new habits form increasingly strong neural connections that overshadow the old addiction connections. Thus, by changing their focus and practicing new behaviors, addicts can jump-start changes in neural processes that push them toward the life they want to lead. In fact, studying the many instances in which this happens helped Lewis formulate his theory that addiction is not a disease from which people can recover. In his experience, those who truly beat addiction move forward to become someone they want to be, rather than recovering or reverting back to the person they were before becoming an addict. "Instead of recovering, it seems that addicts keep growing, as does anyone who overcomes their difficulties through deliberation and insight,"[39] Lewis writes.

Psychological and Behavioral Treatment

To help with complete recovery or sobriety, most psychotherapists administer some variation of what is known as cognitive behavioral therapy to help addicts permanently change their ways of thinking, coping, and behaving. As Akikur Mohammad puts it, "When it works properly, psychological therapy empowers the patient to be her own gatekeeper so she doesn't have to be told (or scolded or shamed) into avoiding behavior that can trigger relapse."[40]

Since addiction governs everything an addict does, a major part of cognitive behavioral therapy focuses on enhancing pastimes that are unrelated to the addiction. This involves strengthening family and other personal relationships and changing the addict's thinking about the importance of his or her role in life. For example, John was addicted to alcohol and illegal drugs from the time he was fifteen until he turned forty-five. He started drinking and using drugs to have fun, but soon his addictions governed his life. He was arrested and jailed more than forty times for theft, selling drugs, driving under the influence of drugs, and other crimes. Finally, at age forty-five, he realized that unless he changed his ways of thinking, he would continue throwing away his life. He received counseling and taught himself to replace his thoughts about going to bars and partying with thoughts of who and what he truly wanted to be—a decent, productive individual. He started college, began caring for his terminally ill mother, and nurtured a positive relationship with his daughter and grandchildren. In his words, "Eventually, staying clean and sober had become the most important thing in my life, more important than having fun."[41]

For Grinspoon, the long process of recovery was initially hampered by his excuses for his behavior; he blamed his stressful job and marriage for his actions. Indeed, many doctors who develop drug addictions start taking these substances to deal with the long hours during medical training (sometimes thirty-six hours straight at a hospital) and with the emotionally stressful aspects of seeing patients suffering and dying. Gradually, Grinspoon realized through psychotherapy that he was responsible for his behavior and had to change. Changing his thinking helped him achieve sobriety and resist the ongoing temptations he knew he would face for the rest of his life. "Over time, the pills sing to me less, but if I listen carefully they still quietly beckon,"[42] he writes. He finds the strength to stay away from the drugs by reminding himself that being allowed to practice medicine and being with his children are more important.

In many treatment programs cognitive behavioral therapy is just one of several forms of therapy offered to recovering addicts.

Another is contingency management therapy, which introduces various types of reward systems for remaining in therapy and conscientiously taking any medications the doctor prescribes. A third is motivational enhancement therapy, which helps addicts maintain their motivation for staying sober. Many programs also include family therapy to strengthen interfamily relationships and to help family members contribute to the addict's recovery in productive ways. Sometimes family members are treated for codependence (behaving in ways that support an addict's addiction); in other cases they are educated about the importance of emotionally supporting a recovering addict.

Informal Treatment

Therapy for families and addicts often includes informal self-help and support groups like Narcotics Anonymous or Al-Anon instead of or in addition to treatment by medical doctors and mental health experts. Psychologist Barbara Sinor and her husband, for example, enabled their son Rich's alcoholism by constantly bailing him out of jail, but after attending Al-Anon meetings, they

Family members often enable addicts by bailing them out of jail or assisting with other problems. Some people realize this is not the best way to help their loved one and begin to seek help themselves to learn how to cope with the addict.

finally realized they could not continue to let Rich ruin their lives. Although they found not being able to help their son devastating, they chose to rescue themselves from the pit of his addiction by not seeing him unless he was sober.

Self-help and twelve-step support groups also work well for some addicts. Sometimes judges in the so-called Drug Courts order nonviolent addicts to attend meetings of these groups in exchange for staying out of jail. These programs are based on total abstinence from addictive substances and behaviors. At the core of programs like these is the notion that addicts are powerless to resist the substances unless they completely stay away and rely on group sponsors and a higher power (such as God) to help them stay sober. Some groups advocate abstinence from any sort of drugs, including those used to treat addiction or other diseases. This is very controversial; indeed, many doctors criticize Narcotics Anonymous in particular for its hard-line stance against therapeutic medications.

Ongoing Treatment

For many addicts, treatment with medication, psychotherapy, and/or support groups must be lifelong to prevent relapses. This is known as aftercare. Even after years of recovery, in some cases environmental cues related to the former addiction, such as someplace where the addict bought drugs, are enough to trigger a relapse.

No matter what forms of treatment addicts undergo, most experience relapses at some point, and many restart treatment many times before finally achieving sustained recovery. Richard, for example, struggled with addiction to cocaine for decades and went through fifteen stints in rehabilitation but kept relapsing. Like many addicts, only after hitting rock bottom—being homeless, jobless, having his mother refuse to give him money, and contemplating suicide—did Richard truly commit to succeeding. With the help of caring professionals, he completed rehabilitation and stayed sober, enrolled in college, and earned undergraduate and graduate degrees in psychotherapy. He became an addiction counselor who loves his job and who often uses his own experiences to encourage addicts not to give up.

Others never succeed in overcoming their addiction. Rich, who became an alcoholic in high school, saw several therapists and tried twelve-step programs but kept relapsing. The medical conditions brought on by his alcoholism, including ulcers, pancreatitis, high blood pressure, liver disease, brain damage, and frequent blackouts, finally killed him at age forty.

Some addicts do achieve sustained sobriety but relapse in response to stressful circumstances. Kat, for example, who had multiple substance addictions, stayed sober for seven years after completing rehabilitation but relapsed after discovering that the man she thought was her biological father was not. The shock led to emotional pain that she began blocking with heroin. She nearly died from overdoses numerous times, and soon neurological damage from the drug caused her to have frequent seizures. However, no rehabilitation facilities would accept her after several failed attempts, because she refused to stay off the drug.

The Search for Permanent Solutions

Researchers are looking for more effective treatment methods to increase the number of addicts who recover permanently. Some researchers are studying whether adding employment counseling and housing assistance to the psychological counseling recovering addicts receive helps prolong recovery. Scientists also seek to develop therapeutic drugs that help addicts deal with various phases of withdrawal and drugs that treat specific forms of addiction. For example, research by University of California–San Francisco professor of neurology Dorit Ron has found that defects in a gene that regulates the production of a chemical called brain-derived neurotropic factor (BDNF) leads to abnormally low levels of BDNF. This in turn dramatically raises the risk for binge drinking and alcoholism. Ron believes that developing methods of increasing BDNF levels in at-risk people might prove to be an effective way either to prevent or treat alcoholism.

CHAPTER 5

Personal Struggles

What is life like for an addict? Some addicts say their lives are a complex combination of extreme highs and extreme lows. Many days they feel as though their lives are out of control—and far beyond their control. They live with feelings of shame, self-loathing, fear, hopelessness, helplessness, loneliness, emptiness, and desperation. They feel trapped in a cycle of trying to fill an empty internal space, compulsively seeking the next fix, reveling in the temporary relief, and again feeling the mounting desperation when the fix starts to wear off.

A Cycle of Desperation

Former drug addict and NBA player Chris Herren vividly explains in his talks to students how his addiction led him to throw away a promising career, overdose and nearly die four times, and almost lose his wife and children. He notes that although many people think addiction is characterized by occasional rock-bottom incidents, for him, the entire duration of the addiction exemplified this quality. "Addiction is rock bottom," he states. "I had 14 years of rock bottom."[43]

He describes several incidents that typified his life as an addict: leaving his wife and newborn son at the hospital because he needed to get drunk, shooting up heroin to be able to function at his mother's funeral, and standing outside the Fleet Center in Boston in the rain to meet his drug dealer while his family, friends, and fans eagerly waited for him to make his debut with the Boston Celtics inside the arena in 2001. His addictions to alcohol and drugs completely governed his life. These compulsions pushed aside everything else and at one point cost him

$25,000 per month, but he could not stop. "People think that when you're doing drugs you're high all the time, out partying. They think you're having fun," he writes in his book, *Basketball Junkie*. "That's not it at all. You're not having fun. You're in hell. Without the dope I would be 'dope sick.' So sick that I couldn't do anything, couldn't even get up. I'd be in a fetal position. You have the sweats one minute, and you're freezing cold the next."[44]

WORDS IN CONTEXT

dope sick

Experiencing withdrawal symptoms drug addicts face when they stop taking the drug to which they are addicted.

Like Herren, some addicts manage to eventually free themselves from the cycle of desperation by developing an understanding of why they are addicted and working diligently to behave and cope more productively. Daniel, for example, ran, exercised, and

Former heroin addict and NBA player Chris Herren speaks to high school students about the consequences of using drugs. His addiction cost him his NBA career and he nearly lost his life.

wrote blog entries—at all hours of the day and night. These activities got in the way of his schoolwork while in graduate school. When Daniel finally realized what was happening, he worked hard to understand his addictive tendencies and to control his compulsive behaviors before they could take over his life. He realized that he felt an emptiness inside that "will try to feed on anything that gives me an instant sense of self-definition, purpose, or worth." Once he understood this, he learned to tame these behaviors by taking responsibility for what he called "my own fear of emptiness"[45] and redirecting his energies toward mindful, rather than compulsive, endeavors.

But self-awareness is not enough for some addicts. Kat, who suffered from numerous substance and behavioral addictions, understood that her childhood experiences and low self-esteem drove her behavior, but she did not succeed in overcoming her compulsions. "I'm addicted to anything I do more than twice and what makes me feel good," she states. "My life then immediately becomes out-of-control and unmanageable . . . with trying to feed the insatiable hole in my soul."[46] She tried to kill herself several times when she realized that nothing would fill that "insatiable hole," but fortunately she did not succeed in that venture either.

Dealing with Stigma

For some addicts, difficulties with understanding and confronting an addiction stem largely from the associated stigma. The stigma has diminished in modern times as more and more people view addiction as a disease rather than as a moral failing. However, stigma remains prevalent enough that most addicts and their families wrestle with feelings of shame. In his book, *Free Refills*, Peter Grinspoon discusses the intense shame he felt after a local pharmacist called police to report him for forging and filling prescriptions for narcotics. His feelings of shame intensified when area newspapers shared the details of how his medical license was

Doctors and pharmacists are held to a high standard of ethical behavior. They need to be vigilant, and if they suspect a patient of abusing drugs or forging prescriptions, they are required to take action.

suspended, how he lost his job, and how prosecutors filed criminal charges against him for endangering patients and violating his medical oath. He also notes that since doctors are viewed as upstanding people who save lives, the stigma that follows those who are addicts is especially harsh. "The media coverage of physicians in distress tends to be lurid and derisive," he writes. "We are held to impossibly high standards, and then . . . when we do fall, we are shunted to the side, sanctioned, stripped of our qualifications, derided, and often deprived of the chance to be healed."[47]

Stigma affects all types of addicts—not just drug addicts. For example, when twenty-three-year-old British accountant Joshua

For Some Addicts, Addiction Is All They Know

Addiction leads many people to forsake their roles as responsible parents, students, employees, or other functions. But in some cases people are trapped as addicts because this is the only lifestyle they know, and they cannot envision an alternative. For such individuals, recovery requires understanding that it is possible to behave otherwise, along with overcoming the addiction. Jake, for example, who was addicted to opiates and cocaine for more than fifteen years, told his physician he could not quit because "it's part of my every day . . . I don't know how to be without it. . . . You take it away, I don't know what I'm going to do."

Teresa, who grew up with an alcoholic mother and an abusive, marijuana-addicted father, exemplifies an addict who knew only an addict's lifestyle since early childhood. Teresa ran away from home after being sexually molested by male relatives as a teenager. She then became addicted to a variety of drugs while living on the streets or with abusive drug dealers who were just like her father. Like her mother, she nearly died from beatings by abusive boyfriends, and she continued to abuse substances after she became pregnant. After her baby was born, Teresa left the baby with a teenaged babysitter for five days while partying nonstop. Eventually, the courts declared her an unfit mother, which puzzled her because she did not know what a fit mother was.

Quoted in Gabor Maté, *In the Realm of Hungry Ghosts.* Berkeley, CA: North Atlantic, 2010, p. 47.

Jones jumped off an office building balcony and killed himself in July 2015, his father, Martin, stated that Joshua "died of shame"[48] about his gambling addiction. At one point, Jones begged his parents not to tell his employer about his addiction, which led him to borrow the equivalent of about $39,000 to cover his bets. Jones also led a double life in which shame led him to hide his addiction from everyone except his parents and a few close friends. Others knew him only as a hard worker and talented hockey player and musician who was fun to be with.

Stigma and related shame also profoundly affect addicts' family members. Alana Levinson, who studies and writes about this topic, reveals that she, her mother, and her brother "subscribed to an unspoken pact of silence" about Alana's father's drug addiction because of their shame. When Alana was six, her parents divorced and her father was banished from their lives. "I remember, even at such a young age, feeling shame that he was so odd and unpredictable," she writes. "In my upper-middle class enclave, it was embarrassing enough that I had a single mother, let alone a father who was banned from seeing us. I'd go to great lengths to hide my family history. Even into adulthood, I thought my story was uniquely humiliating."[49]

Journalist David Sheff, the author of award-winning books about his son Nic's drug addiction, also states that stigma fuels affected children's reluctance to talk about a parent's addiction. "If a parent had a heart problem or cancer or something like that, it'd be talked about in school with teachers, there would be support, other families would be offering to help with childcare, bringing casseroles over," Sheff says. "But with this problem, because it is perceived to be a problem of choice and morals, the child is shamed. There's no sense of community support and so they're further isolated."[50]

The Power of Addiction

Although the public and even addicts' families tend to view addiction as a moral failing, addicts themselves deal every day with the overwhelming power addiction wields. This power leads addicts to do things they never thought they would do and to literally abandon other parts of their lives to maintain their habit. Canadian physician Gabor Maté works in an inner-city addiction clinic and overcame a personal shopping addiction, so he understands this power on a personal and professional level. As he explains, "People jeopardize their lives for the sake of making the moment livable. Nothing sways them from the habit—not illness, not the sacrifice of love and relationships, not the loss of all earthly goods, not the crushing of their dignity, not the fear of dying. The drive is that relentless."[51]

According to an article in the British newspaper the *Mirror*, Joshua Jones once described the power of addiction by telling his parents that "one time he had been lying on his bed shaking, desperately trying to resist the urge to place a bet."[52] Unfortunately, he was not able to withstand the urge. In fact, his gambling addiction led him to do things that were contrary to his usual behaviors as an intelligent, hardworking young man. While a student at Surrey University in Guildford, England, he spent his student loan on gambling. After that, his parents gave him a small amount of spending money, so he took high-interest payday loans and borrowed money from friends to gamble. He continued this pattern after landing his dream job as an accountant.

The desperation to obtain the next fix also leads many addicts to resort to criminal acts. Often, shoplifting and otherwise stealing goods and money become a way of life because they allow the addict to finance his or her addiction. For example, Mike, one of Maté's drug-addicted patients, stole Maté's mobile device during an appointment when Maté left the room for about twenty seconds. When Maté realized what had happened, he confronted Mike, who calmly stated, "It was there on your desk. What could I do?"[53]

Although Maté initially thought Mike was trustworthy, he notes that this casual acceptance of criminal acts is common among addicts. He thus quickly learned to be careful in his medical practice, even with patients like Mike. "I naively thought that this man, who once made me a finely worked wood carving to express his gratitude, could be trusted. Perhaps he could be trusted, but his addiction could not,"[54] Maté writes.

Ruined Relationships and Lives

The power of addiction also results in many addicts watching their addictions destroy their careers, plans, and relationships. For example, video game addict Ryan van Cleave played *World of Warcraft* for about sixty hours per week. He neglected his job as a college English professor and ignored his wife and children. After he lost his job, his family had little money to live on, his children resented him, and his wife kept threatening to leave him. But he still spent significant amounts of money buying new computers with better game graphics and invested $224 in fake gold so his *World of Warcraft* avatar could wear expensive armor and fight with an expensive sword. Only after he almost committed suicide

A college student plays the online video game World of Warcraft. Both children and adults can become addicted to video games to the point that they flunk out of school or lose their jobs.

did Van Cleave force himself to endure the withdrawal symptoms that allowed him to overcome his addiction. Still, rebuilding his life and finding a new job took several years.

In other situations, a teenager's addiction devastates families and changes the addict's plans for the future. In 2016 fifteen-year-old Derek's frantic parents gave up on taking him to a therapist for his video game addiction because Derek would not cooperate with the therapist's efforts. Derek was previously a bright, hardworking student who got good grades and planned to go to college. His addiction turned him into an angry, combative boy who flunked all his classes, tore his room apart, and threatened his parents when they tried to limit his computer use. But from Derek's viewpoint, his parents and therapist were the ones with the problem.

Numerous cases where video game–addicted parents have neglected their children have also occurred. For instance, in one tragic case three-month-old Sarang died after her parents, Kim Jae-beom and Kim Yun-jeong, let her starve at home while they spent entire nights playing *Prius Online* in Internet cafés in South Korea. Ironically, in this game, players raise a virtual baby that ac-

Passion Versus Addiction

A dilemma that affects many addicts is that sometimes a formerly pleasurable, harmless activity morphs into an addiction, and it is unclear when it is necessary to take steps to control the compulsive behavior. In fact, one reason that addiction expert Gabor Maté is so well qualified to advise patients on this issue is that he overcame an addiction that grew out of a harmless passion for listening to classical music. His enjoyment evolved into a compulsive need to buy hundreds and sometimes thousands of dollars' worth of music CDs a week, followed by a compulsion to hide the CDs and lie to his wife and children about where he had been and what he had done.

The best way to distinguish between an addiction and a passion, Maté writes, is to ask "who's in charge, the individual or their behavior? It's possible to rule a passion, but an obsessive passion that a person is unable to rule is an addiction." In addition, an addiction negatively impacts other aspects of an individual's life. For example, Maté not only lied to his wife and children about his CD-buying sprees but also endangered his children. In one instance he left his eleven-year-old son alone for more than an hour in a comic book shop while he snuck away to buy CDs at a music store. His behavior also led him to hate himself; indeed, he writes, "this self-loathing manifested itself in the harsh, controlling, and critical ways I'd deal with my sons and my daughter."

Gabor Maté, *In the Realm of Hungry Ghosts*. Berkeley, CA: North Atlantic, 2010, pp. 115, 120.

quires magical powers as she grows. The night Sarang died, the parents admitted to police that their gaming session took longer than usual, but they could not leave. Detective Sang Yoon Han, who investigated the case, stated, "A typical parent would weep in this situation, but they showed no emotion"[55] when police arrived at their home. The two were convicted of negligent homicide.

Trying to Quit

The power of addiction is also illustrated by the difficulty of quitting. Many addicts, in fact, try numerous times and fail, and others recover but relapse. Some addicts seem to truly want to quit but cannot overpower the addiction. Joshua Jones, for example, was aware that he needed help and was seeing a therapist and undergoing hypnosis before he killed himself. But his gambling compulsions were so strong that in one instance, he went straight from a hypnosis session to a gambling binge.

Rich, who became addicted to alcohol during adolescence, tried to quit countless times. However, he kept relapsing over the next twenty years because alcohol continued to blot out his anger, frustration, and disappointment with himself, just like it did when he was a teenager. He thus never really wanted to be without it. As a teenager, alcohol erased Rich's embarrassment about his severe hearing loss and speech problems and helped him fit in with peers. It also soothed his distress when his parents divorced when he was twelve. "Just being part of a group was the most important thing to me. Even though I was doing *wrong* things, it didn't matter. . . . When I got buzzed I didn't stutter and people didn't tease me,"[56] he says. Later on, when his doctor warned him that his alcoholism was killing him, he tried to quit with counseling and twelve-step programs. Once he remained sober for three years but subsequently resumed his pattern of relapsing whenever he became angry or disappointed in himself.

Lifelong Challenges

Although many addicts do recover and go on to lead productive, happy lives, the shadow of the addiction always lurks and remains a lifelong challenge. Even people who successfully recover for many years risk relapsing and dying from overdoses and similar mishaps, and this is one of the scariest aspects of addiction for many.

The addiction-associated deaths of numerous celebrities have brought this issue front and center for many addicts and for society as a whole. For instance, when the actor Philip Seymour Hoffman died of a drug overdose in 2014 at age forty-six after being sober since age twenty-two, his fans were shocked. Other recovered addicts were frightened because Hoffman had stayed sober for so long before he started abusing prescription drugs and subsequently began snorting heroin in 2012. "Regardless of how much clean time you have, relapsing is always as easy as moving your hand to your mouth," says science writer and recovering addict Seth Mnookin. "It's impossible to know what led Hoffman to start using after so many years of sobriety. After he opened a portal to that vortex of chemical relief, however, it doesn't surprise me at all that he couldn't heave himself out in time to save his life."[57]

Former addicts who do stay sober learn to constantly push aside any temptation to relapse by embracing the personal connections and productive pastimes that have gained more importance than the addiction. As addiction specialist and talk show host Dr. Drew Pinsky states in his book *Cracked*, "Every one of my patients enjoying successful recovery has discovered that the only way to get past pain, fear, and feelings of powerlessness or insignificance is by connecting with other people. They do it in meetings, with sponsors, with family and friends. Those new relationships are the building blocks of a new life."[58] Still, recovered addicts like Mnookin, who relies on sustaining his status as a married man, father, journalist, and Massachusetts Institute of Technology instructor to keep away from alcohol and drugs,

WORDS IN CONTEXT

clean time
The length of time during which an addict has not engaged in his or her former addictive habit.

know that everything they have built in their lives could easily disappear in a second unless they remain diligent.

For Chris Herren, knowing that he is making a difference by helping young people resist peer pressure and develop productive methods of coping is one factor that keeps him sober. He also regularly attends twelve-step meetings to keep on track. But the strongest motivation for staying clean came when he realized that his proudest achievement was being home to wake his young children up for school every morning and to tuck them into bed at night. For Herren and other addicts who strive to remain in recovery, it is often small but incredibly important milestones like this that help them overcome the lifelong challenges that their addictions bring.

SOURCE NOTES

Introduction: The Personal and Social Impact of Addiction

1. National Center on Addiction and Substance Abuse, "What Is Addiction?," 2017. www.centeronaddiction.org.
2. Substance Abuse and Mental Health Services Administration, "Prevention of Mental Illness," August 9, 2016. www.samhsa .gov.
3. Centers for Disease Control and Prevention, "Health Effects of Secondhand Smoke," January 11, 2017. www.cdc.gov.
4. Association of American Universities, "Executive Summary," *Report on the AAU Climate Survey on Sexual Assault and Sexual Misconduct.* December 14, 2015. www.aau.edu.
5. James P. Gray, *Why Our Drug Laws Have Failed and What We Can Do About It.* Philadelphia: Temple University Press, 2001, p. 9.

Chapter 1: What Is Addiction?

6. Quoted in Samantha Dunn, "Inside Dr. Drew's *Celebrity Rehab*," *O, the Oprah Magazine*, February 2008. www.oprah .com.
7. Quoted in Barbara Sinor, *Tales of Addiction and Inspiration for Recovery*. Ann Arbor: MI: Modern History, 2010, p. 97.
8. Quoted in National Institute on Drug Abuse, "Drugs, Brains, and Behavior: The Science of Addiction," July 2014. www .drugabuse.gov.
9. National Institute on Drug Abuse, "Drugs, Brains, and Behavior."
10. David Sack, "Addiction Is a Disease and Needs to Be Treated as Such," *New York Times*, February 11, 2014. www.nytimes .com.
11. Nora D. Volkow et al., "Neurobiologic Advances from the Brain Disease Model of Addiction," *New England Journal of Medicine*, January 28, 2016, p. 364.

12. Stanton Peele, "Is Addiction a Brain Disease?," *The Fix*, March 16, 2015. www.thefix.com.

13. Maia Szalavitz, "Most of Us Still Don't Get It: Addiction Is a Learning Disorder," Substance.com, July 17, 2014. www.substance.com.

14. Marc Lewis, *The Biology of Desire*. New York: Public Affairs, 2015, pp. xii–xiii.

15. Lewis, *The Biology of Desire*, p. 29.

16. Peter Grinspoon, *Free Refills*. New York: Hachette, 2016, p. 186.

Chapter 2: What Causes Addiction?

17. G.J. Wang et al., "The Role of Dopamine in Motivation for Food in Humans: Implications for Obesity," *Expert Opinion on Therapeutic Targets*, October 2002, p. 601.

18. Ronald Kotulak, *Inside the Brain: Revolutionary Discoveries of How the Mind Works*. Kansas City, MO: Andrews McMeel, 1997, p. 8.

19. Quoted in Sinor, *Tales of Addiction*, p. 11.

20. Gabor Maté, *In the Realm of Hungry Ghosts*. Berkeley, CA: North Atlantic, 2010, p. 36.

21. Michael Nader and Paul W. Czoty, "PET Imaging of Dopamine D2 Receptors in Monkey Models of Cocaine Abuse: Genetic Predisposition Versus Environmental Modulation," *American Journal of Psychiatry*, August 2005, p. 1476.

22. US Department of Health and Human Services, Office of the Surgeon General, *Facing Addiction in America*. Washington, DC: Health and Human Services, 2016. https://addiction.surgeongeneral.gov.

Chapter 3: Prevention of Addiction

23. Quoted in Elaine Korry, "To Prevent Addiction in Adults, Help Teens Learn How to Cope," National Public Radio, November 12, 2015. www.npr.org.

24. National Institute on Drug Abuse, "Drugs, Brains, and Behavior."

25. Amy Nordrum, "The New D.A.R.E. Program—This One Works," *Scientific American*, September 10, 2014. www.scientificamerican.com.
26. Quoted in Penn State News, "REAL Strategies Help Youth Resist Peer Pressure," June 14, 2010. http://news.psu.edu.
27. Quoted in Broadalbin-Perth Central School District, "Former NBA Player Chris Herren Challenges BPHS Students to 'Be You,'" January 14, 2016. www.bpcsd.org.
28. US Department of Health and Human Services, Office of the Surgeon General, *Facing Addiction in America*.
29. Quoted in Korry, "To Prevent Addiction in Adults, Help Teens Learn How to Cope."
30. Quoted in John Tierney, "The Rational Choices of Crack Addicts," *New York Times*, September 16, 2013. www.nytimes.com.
31. Quoted in National Institute on Drug Abuse, "Dr. Thomas Kosten Q&A: Vaccines to Treat Addiction," June 11, 2015. www.drugabuse.gov.

Chapter 4: Treating and Overcoming Addiction

32. National Institute on Drug Abuse, "Drugs, Brains, and Behavior."
33. National Center on Addiction and Substance Abuse, "Addiction Medicine: Closing the Gap Between Science and Practice," June 2012. www.centeronaddiction.org.
34. Akikur Mohammad, *The Anatomy of Addiction*. New York: Perigee, 2016, p. xi.
35. Mohammad, *The Anatomy of Addiction*, p. 11.
36. National Center on Addiction and Substance Abuse, "Addiction Medicine."
37. National Center on Addiction and Substance Abuse, "Addiction Is a Disease," 2017. www.centeronaddiction.org.
38. Maté, *In the Realm of Hungry Ghosts*, p. 387.
39. Lewis, *The Biology of Desire*, p. 115.
40. Mohammad, *The Anatomy of Addiction*, p. 100.
41. Quoted in Sinor, *Tales of Addiction*, p. 74.
42. Grinspoon, *Free Refills*, p. 216.

43. Quoted in Kevin Conlon, "Former NBA Player Recounts Struggle with Drug Addiction," *CNN*, February 24, 2012. www.cnn.com.

44. Chris Herren and Bill Reynolds, *Basketball Junkie*. New York: St. Martin's, 2011, p. 14.

45. Quoted in Maté, *In the Realm of Hungry Ghosts*, p. 231.

46. Quoted in Sinor, *Tales of Addiction*, p. 59.

47. Grinspoon, *Free Refills*, p. 227.

48. Quoted in Laurie Hanna and Steve White, "Tragic Gambling Addict Joshua Jones 'Died of Shame' as His Dad Calls for Crackdown," *Mirror* (London), April 27, 2016. www.mirror.co.uk.

49. Alana Levinson, "Surviving the Secret Childhood Trauma of a Parent's Drug Addiction," *Pacific Standard*, November 20, 2014. https://psmag.com.

50. Quoted in Levinson, "Surviving the Secret Childhood Trauma of a Parent's Drug Addiction."

51. Maté, *In the Realm of Hungry Ghosts*, pp. 29–30.

52. Hanna and White, "Tragic Gambling Addict Joshua Jones 'Died of Shame' as His Dad Calls for Crackdown."

53. Quoted in Maté, *In the Realm of Hungry Ghosts*, p. 297.

54. Maté, *In the Realm of Hungry Ghosts*, p. 296.

55. Quoted in Nina Strochlic, "'Love Child' Game Over: Internet Addicts Let Their Baby Starve to Death," *Daily Beast*, July 21, 2014. www.thedailybeast.com.

56. Quoted in Sinor, *Tales of Addiction*, pp. 25–26.

57. Seth Mnookin, "Why Philip Seymour Hoffman's Death Is So Scary," *Slate*, February 4, 2014. www.slate.com.

58. Drew Pinsky, *Cracked*. New York: HarperCollins, 2003, p. 267.

FOR FURTHER RESEARCH

Books

Michael Centore, *Causes of Drug Use*. Broomall, PA: Mason Crest, 2016.

Cheryl Musick, *The Day the Musick Died: A Mother-Daughter Addiction Journey of Suffering, Loss, and a Ray of Hope*. North Charleston, SC: Create Space, 2016.

Connie Goldsmith, *Addiction and Overdose: Confronting an American Crisis*. Minneapolis, MN: Twenty-First Century, 2017.

Joe Herzanek and Judy Herzanek, *Why Don't They Just Quit?* Berthoud, CO: Changing Lives Foundation, 2016.

John Perritano, *Opioids: Heroin, OxyContin, and Painkillers*. Broomall, PA: Mason Crest, 2016.

Jon Reese, *Drugs*. Broomall, PA: Mason Crest, 2016.

Christine Watkins, *Addiction*. Farmington Hills, MI: Greenhaven, 2014.

Internet Sources

Johann Hari, "The Likely Cause of Addiction Has Been Discovered, and It Is Not What You Think," *Huffington Post*, January 25, 2016. www.huffingtonpost.com/johann-hari/the-real-cause-of-ad dicti_b_6506936.html.

Jack Rodolico, "Anatomy of Addiction: How Heroin and Opioids Hijack the Brain," National Public Radio, January 11, 2016. www .npr.org/sections/health-shots/2016/01/11/462390288/anatomy -of-addiction-how-heroin-and-opioids-hijack-the-brain.

Sally Satel, "Is Addiction a Brain Disease?," *U.S. News & World Report*, May 11, 2016. www.usnews.com/news/articles /2016-05-11/is-addiction-a-brain-disease.

Emma Young, "How Iceland Got Teens to Say No to Drugs," *Atlantic*, January 19, 2017. www.theatlantic.com/health/archive /2017/01/teens-drugs-iceland/513668.

Websites

American Psychiatric Association (www.psychiatry.org). The American Psychiatric Association is a professional organization for psychiatrists, who diagnose and treat mental illnesses, including addiction. Its website contains information about all aspects of addiction.

American Society of Addiction Medicine (www.asam.org). The society is a professional organization for physicians and other professionals who work with people with addictions. The resources section on its website provides the public with information about prevention, treatment, diagnosis, and other aspects of addiction.

National Center on Addiction and Substance Abuse (www .centeronaddiction.org). The National Center on Addiction and Substance Abuse is a nonprofit organization that provides information about the economic, personal, and social costs of addiction and how to prevent and treat addiction.

National Institute on Drug Abuse (www.drugabuse.gov). This government organization seeks to advance scientific studies of addiction to improve individuals' and the public's health. It sponsors and conducts relevant research and educates the public about all aspects of addiction. Its NIDA for Teens site is an interactive website for teens that contains information, along with videos and games, about drugs and addiction.

Substance Abuse and Mental Health Services Administration (www.samhsa,gov). This government agency leads efforts to reduce the impact of addiction and mental illness on communities. It oversees programs, distributes information, and studies substance abuse and mental health issues.

INDEX

PICTURE CREDITS

Cover: iStockphoto.com/CO 2

4: Maury Aaseng

6: Tek Image/Science Source

11: Joseph Sohm/Shutterstock.com

13: George Rudy/Shutterstock.com

16: Creativalmages/Thinkstock Images

23: Huntstock/Thinkstock Images

26: threerocksimages/Shutterstock.com

28: rez-art/Thinkstock Images

34: Jack Hollingsworth/Thinkstock Images

36: Brian Harkin/MCT/Newscom

43: American troops running towards a chopper during the Vietnam War/Universal History Archive/UIG/Bridgeman Images

47: bowdenimages/Thinkstock Images

51: Brian Snyder/Reuters/Newscom

55: sirtravelalot/Shutterstock.com

59: Associated Press

61: Fabiana Ponzi/Shutterstock.com

65: Xu Kangping/FeatureChina/Newscom

ABOUT THE AUTHOR

Melissa Abramovitz is an award-winning author who specializes in writing educational nonfiction books and magazine articles for all age groups, from preschoolers through adults. She also writes short stories, poems, and picture books. Abramovitz graduated summa cum laude from the University of California–San Diego with a degree in psychology and is also a graduate of the Institute of Children's Literature.